No Visible Bruises

NO VISIBLE BRUISES

Diamond

Library of Congress Control Number:		2021925322
ISBN:	Hardcover	978-1-6698-0344-7
	Softcover	978-1-6698-0343-0
	eBook	978-1-6698-0342-3

Print information available on the last page.

Rev. date: 12/10/2021

To order additional copies of this book, contact:
Xlibris
844-714-8691
www.Xlibris.com
Orders@Xlibris.com
835655

CONTENTS

Poems

Preface

There are several people I need to thank for the inception of this book, without whom this book would just be a passing thought.

The first is my psychiatric nurse practitioner, who persuaded me to write this.

Second, I must thank my therapist, without whom I would not be as healed or together as I am today. I now enjoy the fruits of her hard work.

Third, my doctor has had a large hand in my recovery from various illnesses, both physical and mental. He treated me with the expertise of a psychiatrist when I was in between one.

Fourth, I must thank my son because his great need for a healthy mother spurred me to achieve heights that I never thought possible.

Finally, I thank my husband, for without his abiding love, I would not be soaring as an eagle today.

I do want to take this opportunity to thank you for purchasing this book. Because of you, my dream of setting up a nonprofit organization would not be possible. All the proceeds from this book are going directly to this organization. This house will afford women like myself, dually diagnosed (addiction and mental illness), a safe place to stabilize and learn how to live and function.

Again, to all, heartfelt *thanks!*

My pen name is Diamond. I am forty-nine years old, and this is my story.

The Beginning

As far back as I can remember, my brother loomed large over me. He was always the policeman who thumped me because of my being the "robber" or the cat in the cat–mouse game, with me being the mouse. In fact, sometimes you can say that our relationship was like that of the animals we had in our little miniature zoo—always viewing for dominance. We had lots of chickens, a dog, some budgies in an aviary, and a spider monkey, last but not least our aquariums. I should say that it is *his* aquarium, mainly because they were all alive and well, unlike my aquarium, which grew algae well but seemed to be a death sentence to any fish that happened to be in it.

An interesting curiosity was our spider monkey. It had a great distaste for our male nanny; his name was Rajiv. He just happened to be the one elected to feed the monkey. It hated Rajiv for reasons we will never know. The monkey used to bite, hit, and kick Rajiv. Any time Rajiv went near him, Rajiv would end up a stump if he started out as a tree. Often though, we wished that our father would have given us money instead of a couple of nannies and a whole slew of fancy animals. It would have been nice to have a warm full belly.

We grew some food and peppers. The peppers were there because that was how we flavored the rice and a good source of greenery. Straight white rice is not all that appetizing, but when you add some greens and peppers, it starts to taste much better. Mom was always broke because in those days, teachers did not make good money. My mother was an English teacher, so we grew up with two languages in the house and often spoke half English and half Malay.

When I was six, my brother Naim said to me that he was going to do something special for my seventh birthday. I remembered it, all right. I still have nightmares about the movie to this day, though the name has faded. My brother took me to a horror flick when I turned seven! I can still see the mud people in those dark moments. I am not sure if I will ever forgive him for that. All in all, things were good up to the age of seven, granted that sometimes food was a little meager, but we were not starving, if that means something.

Unbeknownst to me, life was going to change beyond repair after my mother met and married husband number two, David Jackson. Just as an aside, husband number one, our father, divorced her. We were not privy to the discussions of who belongs where; we just knew that Mom was not going to be with us anymore. In my heart, I grieved. I missed her. Sometimes I would look out the window, hoping to see her coming back. I always thought that she left because of me, so I started to try to please everybody so that people would not leave me behind again. Some of those times felt very lonely and empty. The things that made my life full were not there anymore.

The other change was that we did not ride the bus anymore. We used the car, equipped with a chauffeur who drove us to wherever we needed to be. We lived in the Sea Park house for a year after Mom left, with just the nannies to take care of us. Even though Rajiv and Omar were our nannies, they became like parents to us because they were always there. Dad left. Mom left, but Rajiv and Omar were always there. In essence, they filled in when our parents were off doing their own thing.

The other shock was the move. We were told that we needed to leave our haven in Sea Park to live with our dad. We were also informed that we had no choice. It felt like the world came crashing about our ears. Dad also told us about what we needed to take, what stayed, and what went into the garbage. Dad had also had us ride his car more than the bus. We accepted it because "what Dad wants, Dad gets." The more we rode the car, however, the more I noticed that Lewis, the chauffer, liked to stare at me. It was kind of unnerving for me at first, but in time, I grew accustomed to it.

Lewis, Dad's Chauffeur — KL, Malaysia

His name was Lewis. He was a short Indian man with a little facial hair, not much. He had a small moustache that was well groomed. He was also soft-spoken. Lewis carried himself with dignity, which I found a convenient front for a predator. One fine day, he asked if I knew what a penis was. I said to him I did not and asked if it was something good or bad. He said that it was a wondrous thing because it could help make babies. I was confused. I thought that Allah made babies and men helped a little in raising a child, but that was about it. So Lewis decided to remedy that by talking to me about sex. Thus began my sex education at the hands of a sexual predator. At first, it was harmless enough. It was just talk, but it did not stay that way. I am not sure what changed, but he became agitated if I did not do the things he asked.

One time, we were in Port Dickson, Malaysia, which is a well-known beach where my father had an apartment. He was tasked to watch my elder autistic stepbrother and me for a night. I don't remember the circumstances, but there we were. It was a two-bedroom apartment. The rooms had an adjoining door. I don't exactly remember how the topic came up, but again, he was talking about the importance of a penis. He said that it could make you feel really good and relaxed. I acknowledged that and was about ready to go to bed when he asked me to lie down flat on the mattress that was on the floor and take off my pants. He wanted to show me something wonderful.

After a little hemming and hawing, I took my panties off and lay flat on my back. He licked the back of his hand and then wet my privates. He said that this was to prepare me for the wonderful thing. Then he beckoned my stepbrother to me and told him to undress. I think you can see where this is going, but Allah be praised, my brother had a meltdown because he was told not to undress in front of strangers, and what Lewis had asked, he did not understand. Both of us felt that it was wrong, except I chose to lie there, while he, not knowing how to deal with any strong emotions, had a meltdown.

In more ways than one, I am grateful for that meltdown. I don't even want to imagine what would have happened otherwise. That, however, was the only opportunity that Lewis had ever gotten for something like that. Allah be praised.

From then on, he would just take my hand and put it on his penis. My body responded to him, which befuddled me. It made me feel dirty, but surprisingly enough, there was an element of joy in it. He would have me masturbate him while he drove. Sometimes I found it thrilling, and others, I just felt wrong. From him, I learned that if you wanted approval like I did, you did whatever was asked no matter what you felt at all times. I was only eight.

Security Guard — KL, Malaysia

At that magic age of eight, my brother and I went to live with my dad. Everything changed. My relationship with my brother morphed into a type of nothingness. Naim retreated into his shell, and me? I seized the opportunity to further develop my people-charming skills to new heights. When Mom left, she took love with her. I felt so deprived in that aspect of my life that the training I had received from Lewis started to seemed good. Lewis made me feel loved, if nothing else.

Shortly after we had moved in with Dad, I hung out in the place where I felt the most desired and comfortable. I was very intimidated by my father's house. To me, it was *huge*. So I started to spend some serious time with the security guard in one corner of the house. One fine day, I was lying on the floor, minding my own business, watching TV, and the security guard came into the room and sat on his cot. He leaned forward and whispered to me that he was going to make those two bumps grow bigger. He said that bigger was better. He put his left hand on his knee; with the right hand, he reached under my shirt and fondled me. I felt cheap and disgusting, but when all was said and done, I went back for more. I was beginning to learn that a good way to a man's heart was sex.

One morning there was a thunderstorm that scared me to no end. I ran to the security guard because to me, he represented safety. He gathered me and took me upstairs. It never occurred to me that this was not a good thing to do. He kept kissing me, and he lowered me to the floor. He reached in between my legs and discovered that I had my period. He then got on top of me and began to masturbate. I felt this penis thing near my vagina, but he never penetrated—thank Allah. Thus, my sex education continued at the hands of another perverted predator.

Penang, Malaysia

One of the things I remember the most about living in Penang was how quiet it was. The humidity was so high that without fail, my skin would crawl and became clammy, slightly sticky. It was like that every day no matter the weather. That year was the first year I discovered a bra. I was taken shopping by my aunt, and she got me about three to four pairs of regular bras because my breasts had developed, far quicker than my mind. I also noticed how my uncle stared at me every chance he got. He would make comments like "You are so pretty" and so on.

I never thought anything of his comments because he was an Imam or an Islamic priest, if you will. My father also told me that I was to receive my religious training from him before I was to go to school in Australia. My father said that he was wrong to have sent my elder brother Naim without the training he needed. So he was going to rectify that with me.

My uncle coughed as the day turned to night every night, it seemed. The fans in my room were on full blast; otherwise, I would have sweated to death from the heat. I could hear the faint creaking of wood underneath big feet. He always made the first floor of the wooden house creak. The door squeaked open—the outline of a male figure came into view. I was not terrified because I knew him. His distinctive cologne wafted into my nose. He meandered to my bed. I asked if everything was okay because a man should not be visiting a young girl's bedroom at night. He cleared his throat noisily and then lifted my nightgown at the same time.

He ran his big chubby fingers all over my stomach, and then moving upward from the stomach, he played with the breasts. In response to his administrations, my lips thickened, nipples erect. My vagina was moist, and the pubic hair was wet. I gasped as he climbed on top of me. I could not breathe. The sheets and bed were dripping with my blood. Everything was red, including me. He snorted every time he moved like the mindless bull he represented. Soundlessly, I screamed. When he was done, I cleaned up and took a shower. I did not know at the time, but he came every other day.

My aunt once asked me what the creaking from my room was all about. I lied and told her that I was dancing to Michael Jackson. Boy, I loved MJ. I even got an afro because of him. Not just that, but also, I won third place in a dancing competition to his song "Thriller."

A lot happened in my ninth year. My uncle was not the only one who took advantage of me. My three cousins did too. Two, Rosman and Rosmin, were brothers from the same family, and the third was my second cousin, Bahar. At this juncture, I would like to qualify that not all of what had happened in Penang was traumatic, even if the majority of events were bad, but at the time, I did not know it was bad until much later. I remember playing soccer with the village kids. I had no idea how much time I spent up our guava tree. I was up that tree every chance I got. The tree and I had a bond because nothing bad ever happened when I was up that tree, so I spent a lot of time up it.

Other than my uncle, the one who was as damaging to me was my second cousin Bahar. He was a favorite among us kids, save Rosman. Everybody loved Rosman more than anything, and Bahar was a close second. The girls especially loved Bahar. We thought he was a handsome man indeed. He had a smile that turned your heart to mush. Whatever Bahar wanted, Bahar got, and us kids made sure of that. When my Aunt told us that he was coming to Penang, us kids went crazy. He would tell us stories about his adventures, and there were lots of oohs and aahs as well as excitement that seemed to break every rule in the house.

He came into the common area. There was a ripple of "He is here! He is here!" with gusto and chanting of his name. He paused in front of me and said that I looked good. He reached over and gave my belly a squeeze. He sat us all down and proceeded to tell us his latest adventures. We hung on every word he said.

The dinner bell went off, and we all got cleaned up. Then it became a waiting game for us. The other game we invariably played, without fail, was musical chairs. Everyone tried to get the seat closest to Bahar. Normally, the older ones got talking, and they also got the best seats in the house.

Regularly, there was very little conversation at the dinner table because everybody was preoccupied with eating and food, but that night was special. Everybody was talking to Bahar and how they had thought that his soon-to-be ex-wife was very unfair and a bitch. Bahar almost choked at the mention of his wife. He was visibly shaken.

I felt sorry for him. I knew that I wanted to make him feel good if not better than before he got to my Aunt and Uncle's place. There was one thing I learned—"The way to a man's heart is sex"—although at the time, I did not know that was what it was called. Sex to me was something my uncle did instead of me identifying it without judgment. I thought hard for a few minutes. Then I realized that I could do what my Uncle did, and Bahar would be "made better."

I waited until darkness fell before I changed. I selected my best nightgown—the one that my Uncle really liked. As soon as it was dark enough, I made my way to his room. Everything sounded so loud, every creak and squeak. As I got to his room, I paused. In that moment, I realized what I was about to do. I hated sex, or at that time, I referred to it as "pleasing men." He was so broken up that I thought the only way to help him was to *please* him. So I opened his door.

I looked at him, and he stared back at me without much thought. He started to say something but fell silent. I had slipped the nightgown over my head, and I heard a gasp from him. Quickly, I made my way to his bed and climbed in. Like all the times with my uncle, I lay real still, waiting for him to screw me, but it was not like that this time. He did not clamber on like my uncle, so I did the next thing I could think of—grab his penis, just like my uncle would take my hand and put it on his penis or Lewis, for that matter. That did it, so I lay real still. Hands snaked around everywhere on my body. Like my Uncle, he got up and went to the restroom. I scampered to my room, pausing only to feel dirty, but I made sure I buried that feeling. I was only ten.

As my tenth year drew to a close, I finally heard from my father. He was taking us kids to Australia to go to school. I did not know whether to be happy or sad. All I knew was Malaysia, either KL or Penang. I felt a strong sense of dread, but with great precision, I stuffed that feeling inside too. I got very good at pushing aside negative things and moved on to better things. It was not easy to do that, but I found that if I did it often enough, my reality would split, and things would get easier to deal with.

There was many a night when I lay awake thinking of the trip to Australia. That was the whole reason why I was in Penang to begin with. My father wanted us to get some religious training from my Uncle before we went to Australia. He said that the school we were going to was a good school, but it was a Christian school. As far as I was concerned, it did not make any sense because I had never met a Christian. I knew about Hindus and Chinese people but not Christians. The only Christian I had ever met at the time was our stepfather, but he was an ex-Christian. He became Muslim when he married our mother. He was the reason why my mother went away from my brother and me.

There was one thing I had learned from my Uncle: people can hold many faces. He was revered by many as an Imam, but to me, he was a snake and a liar. Unbeknownst to me, he was instrumental in my developing different personalities to help me cope with untenable and difficult occurrences.

My eleventh year was uneventful; something was making my Uncle sick, so he did not come to me as often. That did not hurt my feelings one bit. One day I came home from school and found a letter from him addressed to me. I opened it. It simply said, "If you love me, you will get me my cologne for my birthday." I did and left it for him. I did it openly because my Aunt was away in KL.

Soon after his birthday, I got word from my father that he wanted us in KL for some ceremonies involving the Quran because we had finished reading the Quran three times. That was a big milestone for a Muslim kid. It was celebrated by families because it elevated the standing of the family in the community. My Father jumped at the chance to bring together the whole family as he displayed his children's perceived brilliance—a feat not many Muslim kids achieve. Hence, my Father's ego grew akin to the size of Mount Everest. That was my father for you—any chance to "feel good" or inflate his ego, he was all for. He lavished on things that pleased him but not much else. His kids were an added way to bolster his already inflated ego.

Amid the festivities, we got word that my Uncle fell ill. Everybody was up in arms about that, but I could not care less. It was agreed that as soon as the festivities ended, we were to fly to Penang to attend to my Uncle. Shortly after the decision my father had made, my Uncle dropped dead literally. So instead of us nursing him back to health, it became a funeral. Personally, I said, "Good riddance," but I did not share it with anyone at that time.

To this day, I can still close my eyes and see the funeral all over again. I found the funeral worse than the visits I had endured. We kids were not allowed to see the funeral ordinarily, but in my case, they made an exception because "I was so close to him and loved him so much." So my mind imprinted a distaste for funerals. I did not care for him, but I was taken aback at how Muslims treat their dead. He was mummified and literally dumped into the ground—no casket, nothing. I still have nightmares about that to this day.

Geelong, Australia

I was twelve years old when I went to Australia. I stayed at a boarding school called Geelong Grammar School, the Corio campus. I felt free and scared at the same time. I was filled with wonder because of the sea of white faces I saw. I knew what a white man was because of my stepfather, but I never knew there were so many of them all in one place. There were many firsts in the school. It was the first time that there were no visible adults other than the house masters and mistresses. I had to learn how to make a bed properly. I learned about pranks. My peers decided that I was "Ms. Goodie Two-Shoes," so they pranked me.

One day, unbeknownst to me, the girls got together and short-sheeted my bed. I did not know what was going on because the girls were all whispering behind my back, and when I turned around, they would be quiet. They figured out that my hearing was not good. When night fell, I *tried* to get into bed, I could not. The whole floor hooted and hollered, especially when they heard the very audible thud of me falling out of bed. It took me a moment to figure out that I had to remake my bed. As I was making my bed, I could hear the gales of laughter. I felt bad and dumb. Tears were threatening to escape my eyes, so I climbed into bed and pretended that I was asleep. Silently, tears flowed down my cheeks as I faced the wall. There were three of us in a room together.

One night I was sleeping and was woken up with a start. There were noises and shouts everywhere.

One of the older girls woke me up and said, "It's time."

The first thing out of my mouth was "Is it morning already?"

She said no, but it was time for the initiation. She told me what I had to do. I was supposed to run from my boarding house to the tree and back just in my bra and underwear. She said that there was a catch. We were not doing it alone. All the boys were out, and their job was to rip off the girls' underwear and bras.

I felt like a fish out of water. Even at that age, I had no trouble being naked because I was used to it with all the training I had received in Malaysia. As soon as I stepped outside the dorm, I ran for dear life. It was like navigating through a maze of boys who were just grabbing. At last, I got back to the dorm relatively unscathed. I was one of the lucky ones. Some of the other girls took a beating, with missing underwear, scrapes, and bruises because of the roughness of the boys.

One of the biggest joys in middle and high school was music. Music made life bearable. It gave me an outlet to express some of the negativity that I felt. I was thirteen at the time, and the biggest thing I remember about the event was the nightmares. It was not a surprise for me to wake up in the wee hours of the morning and be completely drenched in sweat from night terrors as well as my dear brother's mud people. I will never forget the mud people no matter how old I am. Occasionally, I still wake up in cold sweats thanks to my dearest elder brother.

The other thing that occurred at this time was a little depression. Nobody really noticed the kid in the corner staring out the window or into space. A lot of people said that I was deep in thought or I was studious, but the reality was I was depressed. It did not help that I was carrying a lot of mental baggage. Toward the end of my thirteenth year, I was slated to go to Timbertop. I was thrilled, but my dad stepped in.

He said, "No daughter of mine is going to a boyish campus like Timbertop."

Dad got his wish. I went to the Highton campus for a year. He wanted me to be demure, but I was everything but that. I loved to run cross-country and compete in field hockey games and was absolutely thrilled about riding and working with horses. I had a chance to own my own horse, a jumper too. I might have added that to my repertoire, but again, my dad happened.

He said, "No daughter of mine will stoop so low as to get dirty like that."

My dad used to get mad at me because I was so rough-and-tumble. There began my heart-wrenching fourteenth year.

There was one thing everybody missed in that year. At times, I was awake for about two to three days and would go like the Energizer bunny. During these periods, I had high energy, but when it was over, I entered another phase, which was "sit and stare."

When I was asked why I would stare, without fail, I'd say, "I don't know."

Ian Page

There was another event that occurred at that time, and that was Mr. Ian Page. One of the things that happened when I went to Australia was that I was able to leave the negativity behind and be free of the abuse—or so I had thought. Ian happened.

Halfway through my Highton year, I was introduced to my younger half-brother's teacher Mr. Ian Page. He was one of the adults who took care of us kids in the boarding house. One day, however, I found him tearing up in the common room as he watched his kids play Aussie rules. I asked the wrong question—bad mistake on my part because he started bawling and, in between, sobs shared with me that he no longer had a wife anymore and that it was really affecting his son.

I consoled him the only way I knew how. I nuzzled his neck and said, "It's okay," to him.

He stopped crying, looked at me, and reached for my face. I leaned in and said that everything was going to be all right.

That began a yearlong molestation. I did not know that this was wrong; all I knew was that it made him feel better, so I continued to kiss him, and he used to take pleasure in waking me up with a kiss. This was innocent enough until my father decided to invite him home to our house to thank him for helping my brother Hazreek with his schoolwork. In our house was the first time he made real moves toward me. Our dad's house was a huge house. There were three floors, and you could get lost in them. You could scream on the ground floor and not hear anything on the first floor. This fact led to lots of fondling. He never had intercourse with me, but what he did, however, left a sour taste in my mouth. As far as I was concerned, I did not blame him, only that it happened.

At the end of my fourteenth year, I was not sorry to see the Highton campus go. I then rejoined the kids coming back from Timbertop to the Corio campus. This was where I met the first *real* holy man I ever knew. His name was Father Pash. With him were his wife and two kids. He was a Church of England priest. He was also progressive in his view. He took me under his wing, even though I was a Muslim at that time. He knew that I was interested in music, so he asked me to be in his choir, and I loved it. I ended up in the church choir, the church chamber choir (this was where the musicians ended up), and the school choir. I was also in the school band with my trusty "Buddy," my flute. Then once a year, I would be in the school play. I loved it. Those were the only times I felt right. Life hurt too much otherwise.

Even at that young age, I had not only trauma but also an illness. I never thought I was quite right. I always had bouts of sadness and despair. Nobody ever noticed because I would either hide in my room or plaster a smile on my face. Sometimes I felt like the Joker in Batman with the everlasting grin smeared across his face. There were also times when I felt like the Energizer bunny; I kept going and going and going. The other thing I noticed was the intensity of my feelings. I never felt anything in moderation. It had always been highs or lows, with nothing in between. I never knew what "happy" meant until I met my very first "boy" friend. I did not fall head over heels in love. Our love grew over time. His name was Michael Geddes, and I was fifteen.

Then there was a problem. The color of my skin became an issue. The girls were more accepting than the boys. The girls just ignored that; I had a boyfriend. They did not talk about it; nor did they say anything to Michael. The boys, however, were not as nice. There were many times when Michael would show up stiff from bruises that were inflicted by his fellow housemates. The boys were also much more vocal than the girls. I did not know how many times I was referred to as the "black knob" or "Abo" (short for Aborigines). I found myself numb to name-calling.

Because of my special relationship with Michael, I became appointed the position of Minority Rights Activist. It was a long two years. The only thing that made it bearable was Michael. Groups of key boys and girls were brought together by the school principal to facilitate talks and education within the school to raise awareness of the existence of a growing minority community. The prejudice and racism was not restricted to only at school. My father referred to Michael as my "puppy love," nothing to worry about, but he had a long talk with me about marrying the right one in Malaysia. He also talked to me about a couple of boys who came from good families who would make good husbands. My father would make wisecracks about puppy love. My father never figured out that all he was doing was alienating me more.

By the end of my sixteenth year, my father, uncles, and aunts managed to teach me how to hate. I never knew what hate or dislike was until then because you must learn what it is like to love to understand hate. I cherished the time I spent with Michael, even though I knew it was coming to an end. Michael was offered a position in Japan to teach English as a second language. He accepted it because he wanted to take some time off from school because of the plans we made to meet each other at college in Melbourne University, located in the state of Victoria. He was going into the computer science field, and I was going into nursing.

That, however, was never meant to be. We split up in my seventeenth year after my father pushed me to study like him when he was in my position. After the first semester, we were told to take it easy because from the second semester onward, there was no rest. The stress was growing. All the teachers agreed that after the first semester, the work was endless. You were expected to study all the time. Then my father decided to step in and show how his daughter was better than my stepsister to my stepmother. The rat race began in earnest. During my first semester break, I tried to relax, but my dad disagreed with my approach. He wanted me to study *all* the time. So to get him off my back, I did just that. I ate and slept biology, math, chemistry, human development, and society as well as physics. By the end of the first semester, I was burnt out. The other thing I noticed was at times, I would not sleep much, or I would sleep *a lot*. There were no in-betweens. I was either completely wounded or absolutely fine and nothing bothered me.

I found that to survive the trauma of the separation between Michael and me, I had to separate Malaysia and Australia. Both represented two different things to me, a world apart. Never the twine shall meet. When I was with Malaysians, I would be aware that I was more demure, more covered, and pray a lot. When I was in Australia, there was one wonderful word: *freedom*! This schizoid way of looking at things became the basis of an illness that ripped the very fabric of my sanity.

Two-thirds of the way through my seventeenth year (the last year of high school), my father did a heinous act. He put on a *kenduri* in our home in Australia. A *kenduri* is the Malaysian way of giving thanks and sharing your wealth with the community as well as prayers. In my head, when I was in Malaysia, I was the dutiful, prim and proper Muslim daughter of a wealthy, well-respected, old deep-rooted family, much like the Kennedys of the United States, but when I was in Australia, I had freedom and was devoted to the Church of England or Anglican sect within the Christian faith. There was a very clear line in my mind. So one fine day, my father decided to bring Hazreek (my younger half-brother) and me back to our Australian home. He said that he had a surprise for us waiting at the house. It was a surprise, all right. When we walked into the house, it was transformed into a mini Malaysia. Then when I stepped outside, I was in Australia.

The whole thing crashed my brain. I was going through a cascade of failure, and the walls that I so carefully erected to separate the hurtful memories from the good ones came crumbling down. In my confusion, I asked a friend of my father, a Chinese man, to get me a bottle of antihistamine for my cold. He gave me the bottle, and I grabbed a glass of orange juice to take them. I went upstairs to my room and took a couple. For some reason, I kept staring at the bottle and the pills that were in it. Something snapped in my head, I heard the chanting going on below. I looked out the window, and it was still Australia. With tears rolling down my face, I took the rest of the bottle. There began my love affair with pills. I even wrote a poem about it.

Something broke inside me. I think it was my will to live that emerged out of the rumbled chaos. I called to my stepmother, knowing that she would hear me. I collapsed. From then on, my memory is sketchy. The welcomed darkness took hold of me. Apparently, my father took me to the hospital, but I did not remember much of it other than they made me drink liquid charcoal so that I would puke. That was the only memory I have of the hospital and subsequent stay there.

The other thing that happened about the same time was that I found wine coolers and hard ciders. I loved them. I would break out of my shell when I drank. I became Super Liza, and all was well. My father talked with the school and put me in counselling. I have no real recollection of this other than a couple of things that the psychiatrist who treated me believed in. He held the position that medication was the absolute last resort and that talk therapy was a cure-all. As a direct result, I drank as much as I could when I could.

My teachers told my father that I would never graduate high school. I proved them wrong. I passed the exams even though I had missed half the year. I was disappointed because now I was not able to meet Michael in college. That ended my stay in Australia, even though a few people told my father not to do it, but he took me home to Malaysia anyways.

I realize that I have not talked much about my mother. That is because she had no control over what had happened to my brother and me. We visited her and my stepfather yearly for Christmas vacation. Wherever they were, we went there to visit them. Consequently, we got to go to the different countries where they lived. The vacations were a relief for me. The only part I did not care for was that many a night, my mother would get into these black moods. I really disliked that because after, I talked her "up" even when I was experiencing deep despair.

Malaysia — The Second Time

I did not want to go back to Malaysia, but I did not have a choice. I was done with high school, so my father brought me home even if I did not look upon it as home anymore. I also came to the conclusion that there was no way in hell I could marry Michael. So back to the drawing board I went. I was then introduced to a boy named Shazman. We got along good and all, but I always thought that there was an aloofness about him, like he was better than the average guy. His parents approved of our relationship, and my parents liked him as well. It was a match made in heaven—so I thought.

I was also hitting another problem. My sad times were no more. They were replaced with blackness that was so dark that even a torch would not have provided light. The other part of it was that I would have periods of elation that no money or anything could match. Shaz always said that my behavior reminded him of a girl he dated in Florida, USA. I asked him to clarify. He said the girl had "bipolar." This was the first time I had heard of the term. I scoffed at him and said that I was nothing like that. Of course not—nothing that two and a half bottles of tequila a night couldn't fix. That was my life; by day, I was the perfect little angel, but by night, I was a hellion with a need for alcohol.

Alcohol became my mood stabilizer. When I was down, I drank, and when I was up, I drank even more. Shaz also noticed a change in my personality. He used to say that I would be like a different person every time the wind blew. Shaz also noted that my "friends" were not whom he would pick, and he was right. I surrounded myself with a biker gang, from which there was an endless supply of alcohol. I never did drugs, but Lord only knows why, not because that was as available as alcohol was. This was when I took up smoking too. I wanted to be cool. Shazman was not wrong about me; nor was I him. We dated each other because it was so convenient, not because we really loved each other.

Meanwhile, I started to go to college. I entered a twining program with Sunway College. I would go to school there for two years in Malaysia and then to Western Michigan University (WMU) for my final two years in the United States. It seemed like a good idea at the time, just like consuming as much alcohol as possible. Shortly after I had begun college, I sank into a depression so intense that to stay alive, my brain shut down partial motor functions; in other words, I could not walk. I was confined to a wheelchair. My father was distraught. How could his precious daughter be paralyzed? He talked to the doctors and commenced a barrage of testing. I was poked and prodded, and whatever tests that you can think of were performed. The result? Nothing. I was deemed healthy, but nobody could figure out why I could not walk. Because of my father's status, nobody even suggested mental illness.

I kept going to school despite the state of my mental health. One day I was looking in the mirror. I could almost perceive an audible snap. Then I heard a voice that said, "Move, damn it!" I knew I could walk again.

I wheeled myself to the nurse's station and got out of my wheelchair. I almost fell because the muscles were a little out of shape, but I was able to walk. The one thing good about my sojourn in the hospital was that I had not been able to drink, but I craved; at times, it seemed like every minute of the day. I realized that behavior had to change as well.

Come the end of my nineteenth year, the goal I had—to finish my degree at WMU, in Kalamazoo, Michigan, USA—was becoming real. I was relieved that my stay in Malaysia was coming to an end. The only real thing I liked about my homeland was the availability of really good food, but other than that, it was "See you maybe never. Even that might be too soon."

On August 20, 1998, I left Kuala Lumpur, Malaysia, for Kalamazoo, Michigan, USA.

Kalamazoo, Michigan, USA

I arrived here about two days after I had left Malaysia. I felt a dull excitement as I went to the motel I was staying in for a couple of days. As soon as I could, I went to look at an apartment building around the corner from the Western Michigan campus. I checked it out to make sure that it was walking distance or biking distance to the campus. After I was satisfied that it was as advertised, I signed a year's lease with them. Once the flurry of action was completed, everything went quiet. I was not used to living alone. I felt unsafe, not to mention I was still down mood wise with no stability. I also gave up drinking when I came here to the United States, so my illness took over.

I was so lonely in this big beautiful two-bedroom apartment that it was almost unbearable. I decided to get a dog because I was told that they were the best company next to a human. So I scoured the papers for dog ads. The next thing I had to decide on was "What kind of dog?" I did not have a preference, but my brother always said that malamutes made the best dogs. Thus, Snowy came into being. Not really knowing what a puppy farm was, I stumbled across one when I got Snowy. I paid $200 for her, only to find out that she was a genetic mess borne out of uncaring inbreeding. That was the first of many expensive lessons I had learned. The humane society found out about her and wanted to put her down. I told them that if she showed the first sign of her hip dysplasia, I would put her down. They agreed to let me keep her after seeing the bond we had developed.

The other thing I discovered was walking the dog. I would walk Snowy to the WMU pond and bring three loaves of bread to feed the ducks, swans, and fishes. Then I would play hide-and-seek with Snowy. Not to brag, but she always did find me every time no matter where I hid. She knew my smell well. We normally walked at night because then I could let her off the leash, and she could not get into trouble of any kind. I loved it too. It was not dark at all because of the streetlights. The night air was fresh and wholesome.

People v. Kenneth Lyle Simmons III

The Meeting

Snowy needed to go out, and I needed to make a choice: long or short walk? Short it was because I was behind my time. Snowy went on the leash, and out the door we went. The apartment was on the first floor as soon as we got out the main door, Snowy and I both took big deep breaths of the night air. We walked about a block and back.

As I wandered into the bedroom, I heard the door go *click*, and Snowy was barking her head off. I came out of the bedroom to see what Snowy was barking at. I almost crashed right into him. He said hello, and I jumped. I asked him how he had gotten in. He said that the door was ajar, so he just pushed to get in. My response was "Oh." I did not realize that I had not closed the door shut. I did not know how to feel because he acted like a nice guy, but I was a little upset that he had not bothered to knock first. Still, I did not make an issue of it; as far as I was concerned, I thought it was the norm here to do that. So I pushed the feeling of wrongness to the side and just enjoyed his company.

Halloween — The Rape

Two days later, it was Halloween. I got my candy all organized. I was so looking forward to trick-or-treaters. I had never celebrated Halloween before, so I was curious. I also unlocked the door so that the trick-or-treaters would have easier access. I felt so comfortable that it did not occur to me that maybe it was not a bright idea.

I was in the kitchen, cooking dinner. I heard the door swing open. I had forgotten that Snowy was not there to bark at strangers. I heard a laugh and the jingling of keys. I turned and recognized Ken. I asked him how he had gotten in, not thinking that I had left the door unlocked.

His response was "The door was open."

For some reason, my gut was giving me fits, and my senses went on alert. As he advanced, I took a step back. I smelled the stench of dried beer on him and his breath. I tried to take another step back, but I found that I could not because I had hit the wall. He laughed. My heart was pounding like it was going to burst out of my chest. Inside myself, I was screaming, *No!* I was against the wall when he pressed his body on me.

He laughed. I will never forget that laugh. He threw me on the floor and undressed me. My mind was screaming, but my body just took it. I responded to him the way I had done with my Uncle and Bahar. I lay there as he entered me. My emotions were so tremulous that my vision went black, like when you are going to pass out. The other strong emotion I felt was numbness, if you can call it an emotion. One other thing I noted was that my skin was clammy. When he was done, he laughed and left. I found myself "coming to" and on the floor naked. I got up and took a shower and scrubbed myself until I was pink. Then I sat down, numb. I called the crisis line and told them. Though I did not call it rape, the lady on the phone called it that. I did nothing, not wanting to rock the boat.

The Trial

A day later, I heard this loud banging on the front door. I thought I needed to get to the door. The banging continued. I thought, *Who is it?* I yelled for the person to hold on a minute, that I was coming.

Then I heard his voice saying, "*Open the door, Diamond! I am not playing a fool! I need my keys! Open the door!*"

I called the police. I was referred to a detective. I talked with him, and he said that he was coming to my apartment. I told him how to get there. Soon after the call, there was a soft knock at the door. He came in. He showed me his badge and sat down. I told him what had happened.

He picked up the phone and called the DA. He told the DA what had happened and mentioned that I had a kitchen knife next to me against the wall. The DA told the detective to take me to the hospital to gather evidence. I did not understand this, but I followed the detective because he seemed to know what he was doing.

The one thing I have to say about both was that they were plenty angry. In fact, they were angry enough for me. My prevailing emotion was numbness. The detective also told me that Kenneth was apprehended and that I was safe. My answer was a dumb nod and more numbness, but I did start to relax a little. Then off we went to the hospital.

The doctor asked about the incident. I told him. He collected evidence, like hair and an internal pelvic swab looking for semen and so on. The doctor and detective spoke outside the door of my room. Then the detective came in, and he was very happy. He said that we had a rock-solid case and that the DA was handling this one personally. He also said that I would meet her, and she would want to hear my story from me, not just the detective. All I did was nod. Things were spiraling out of my control.

A month later, I went to trial. The detective took me to court. The DA was already there. I was seated to the right of the judge, and Kenneth was on the left. The witness stand was in front of Kenneth. The prosecution then called me to the stand. I walked up, feeling like I was in quicksand, sinking by the second. Time felt like it stood still. The DA questioned me. I maintained my composure, but inside, I was a mess. The DA asked me to identify my assailant. I stood and pointed to the defendant. I then walked back to the seat beside the DA. We broke for an hour.

When the hour was up, the judge informed us that Kenneth had pleaded no contest in exchange for a lighter sentence. He also said that we were going to adjourn for now and meet back in a month. I was tensed and very numb.

The Sentencing

After the month was up, a friend took me to court. The judge stepped into court, and we all stood. The judge then sat, and so did the rest of us. I was incapacitated. The judge started talking. He asked if the defense had anything to add; then he looked in our direction and asked the same thing. We rested our cases. The judge looked at both of us in turn. He announced the sentence. He paused for a moment and said that this court accepted the plea of no contest.

"Kenneth Lyle Simmons III is hereby sentenced to prison for one year without the possibility of parole and subsequent probation for five years."

I felt like somebody had hit me upside the head. My senses were deadened. I got up and met my friend in the audience. She took me home. I opened the door and literally fell in. My vision blurred as I was falling. I passed out. My emotions were intense. I did not understand why everybody who was connected to the prosecution was angry. The only one who was not angry was me. I felt sorry for Kenneth. The other predominant feeling, if you can call it that, was numbness. Somehow I managed to bury the whole thing inside.

Robert Frank Jonaitis Jr.

The Beginning

Shortly after the trial, I started to drink again. I tried not to look at the fact that I broke the promise I had made to myself in Malaysia. The promise was that I was not going to drink again here in the United States. Geographical cures normally don't work, and I was no exception.

One day I had had enough of life. So I went to my favorite bar, called Up and Under, in downtown Kalamazoo, Michigan. I did not pick him; he picked me. He and I ended up sitting side by side at the bar. He said hello, and I responded in the same way. He bought me a drink, and we ended up chatting as well as drinking together until the bar closed. He asked me for a date, and I said yes. I did think he was cute.

We dated for two years and ended up getting married in the third year. We did have lots of good times and awesome memories.

In the Middle of It

We found a place to rent and call home. We needed to move in together. We agreed that we were wasting money in paying two bills of everything. The day came for him to move in; I was going to help him move. I went over to his place and found him drinking. He asked me to do a lap dance for his friend/roommate. I mumbled a no.

Then I said to him, "Why do you want to sell your wife?"

He shrugged. My voice went up an octave. I stated that I was taking the cat I gave him for his birthday. He said that I could not have the cat. I picked up the cat anyways. I made my way to the door. He screamed at me to put it down. Then he lunged at me and grabbed me. He proceeded to throw me against the wall repeatedly. I started to struggle. He had gripped my upper arm until it was black and blue. He did not stop. He kept pushing me against the wall. I started to struggle with him; then he let me go so quickly that I had to make sure that the cat was all right before I left. To this day, I could feel his hands on me. I went back home and went to bed.

The next morning, I stirred, and I was stiff. I tried to swing my legs out like I normally did, and I was greeted with acute pain. I slowly and gently got out of bed. I looked at myself in the mirror and felt like a stranger was looking back because I could not recognize myself because of the bruises. Some of the bruises were bad enough that they swelled.

The End of Husband Number One

There was one thing that was clear about Rob: I was afraid of him. The above was the very first incident. There were many more bruises and rapes. Sometimes he would come back home after drinking and want sex. He would find me and do it wherever in the house whether I wanted to or not. Nobody knew the horror because I would always have a half smile plastered on my face, but there was one person who saw past the charade.

Dennis the Savior

I met Dennis in the Alano Club in Kalamazoo, Michigan, at an AA meeting. He impressed me with his many years of sobriety. I also thought that he was very handsome and well groomed.

We were friends for one year then things changed. We went to an AA dance together, one of many, but this one was different. We talked and danced and then conversed more. We enjoyed ourselves immensely. It was like time stood in suspended animation. It was such a novel experience for me. For the first time since Michael Geddes, I was ill at ease with a man. The attraction between us was strong. We were dancing three feet away from each other, but we might as well have been glued because of the attraction and electricity passing between us.

After the dance, we sat together and chatted. I think Dennis was tired of the mixed messages and barrier that I put up between us. He stated rather tartly that if I was so happily married, why did I go to the dance with him instead of my husband?

"I think you are anything but happy," he said.

I was flabbergasted. He was right. I could not take the shoving anymore. I went home, packed my bags, and left for Dennis's house.

That night, we made love for the first time. We found out that we matched each other sexually as well. He saw the bruises that had not healed, yet I could tell by the look on his face what he thought of them. By this time, I was high and very manic.

Dennis was a kindhearted person. With his care, I went into counselling to deal with the ghosts of past years. I found that no matter where I went or what I did, there I was. I knew that I could not get better without looking at the past that shaped me. I found myself surfing the net often. I met a therapist online named Thomas Edward Rifenberg. He wanted me to leave Michigan and join him in New York, on the Erie Canal in Port Gibson.

I was torn. I hated Rob with a passion, loved Dennis with every fiber of my being. I talked to Dennis about Thom. It was agreed that for my benefit, I ought to leave for New York to get the help I sorely needed. So I thought, *New York, here I come.* Dennis did not know, however, that I had written his phone number in my diary. I wanted to contact him again when the time was right.

Thomas Edward Rifenberg

I told Thom that I would be in a red dress when I arrived in Rochester, New York. I said that I would have two big luggage cases and a carry-on bag. When I walked out, I stood for a moment, and I saw this older gentleman making his way to me. He introduced himself as Thomas Rifenberg. I blurted out my name and gave him a hug. He kept looking at me. I was getting uncomfortable.

We got into his truck and left the airport. By this time, I was pretty much lost, which was no big surprise; I did not know the area. I did, however, notice that we passed by the same parking lot the third time. I made sure that I shut up so that he would not miss his exit. The drive was uneventful and silent, punctuated by a flurry of words but mainly quiet.

There is one thing I would like to note now before we go any further: overall, I had always had positive feelings for Thom. He guided me with my mental illness, called bipolar. He was insistent that I try therapy and see a psychiatrist. We talked sometimes into the wee hours of the morning. He was a good listener, and I had plenty to say. I had twenty-nine years of stuffing coming out.

He knew of my past. I never sat and shared it with him, but he was a good enough therapist to see the neon signs I would hang right above my head. More than anything else, there was one word that described us, and that was *friends*. Thom and I were best friends. The *one* time we had sex early on in our relationship, I got pregnant and lost the baby at three weeks old. I was distraught and went to the gynecologist. She diagnosed me with grade 4 endometriosis, borderline cancer. The outer lining of my uterus grew outward and attached itself to the broad lateral muscle. Consequently, my ovaries and bladder were stuck to it, and the growth was moving toward my kidneys. The doctor said I needed surgery!

I was crestfallen. Never in my life had I ever faced anything so serious, where life hung in the balance, as then. I made the decision to go ahead. The doctor then removed the growth but could not get all of it. It was suggested that I go through Lupron therapy. It was a therapy that induced menopause, and the theory was that the growth would shrink without estrogen to feed it, and it did. I went through six months of Lupron therapy, and I could have killed Thom a couple of times.

He suggested that by the time I hit menopause, I would be a pro at it because I would have gone through it once already. He was driving me to the hospital when he said this, and I damn near threw him out the door. I was *mad!* The second time he made a similar comment was when I was in a canoe, fishing with him on the wide waters. Sense prevailed, so I did not dump him in the canal the way I wanted to. I did not talk to him for a couple of days though.

At the end of the Lupron therapy, my doctor declared that I was clean. She also suggested that if I wanted to have a baby, now I could. My thoughts when she said that were *Yeah, right! I have not managed to have one to date, so yeah, that is* really *going to happen.*

That night, Thom and I got romantic, and we had sex. I thought nothing of it. A week later, however, I got really sick for really no good reason. I did not have the flu or anything, just felt unwell. So I went to the doctor. I told the doctor how I was feeling, and she suggested that I take a pregnancy test. I scoffed at that but did do it. Lo and behold—I found out I was pregnant. Then I got scared.

I realized that I had to take better care of myself—if nothing else, for my baby's sake. I came off *all* medications, both over the counter and prescription. I told Thom that he was going to be a dad.

He nonchalantly said, "Good. About time."

I did not know how to feel about that, so I ignored it. I was told to use lotion to keep the skin supple because of the stretching. I did. I used a form of shea butter. Every day I would rub it into my belly. Then I observed that I was getting itchy to itchier and worse. One day I looked at my belly, and I was covered in rashes. All the places that I rubbed the lotion on were encased in red welts. Thom never helped me with the rash except for telling me how to care for it. I felt alone and lonely. The burden of his heart disease was weighing on me too. I wondered if my baby would know his/her father. Thom had twelve stents in his heart.

At three months pregnant, I talked to a retired police officer. She said that the law states that if you bear a child while you are still married, the child is considered your husband's, even if the child may not be biologically his. I was mortified. The last thing I wanted was a miniature Robert Frank Jonaitis Jr. I needed a divorce.

Pregnancy–Divorce: The End

The pregnancy was a difficult one. My prenatal numbers were borderline diabetic. I was also anemic. My doctor monitored my blood sugar levels, my mental health, and any other physical ailments that I may have developed, like the reaction I had to prenatal vitamins. They made me so sick that I threw up after taking them. My doctor then gave me iron supplements and regular vitamins. That did not hurt my feelings any.

I was gaining weight. We also moved from Newark, New York, to Speculator, New York, in the Adirondack Mountains. I went to Nathan Littauer Hospital for the pregnancy in Gloversville, New York. By this time, I hated what I looked like. I was a baby elephant. I had never had a belly in all my life until then, and I was *big* because of the pregnancy.

I was six months pregnant when I talked to the divorce lawyer. I told the lawyer about Rob and that I wanted the easiest way out before it was time for me to have the baby. As luck would have it, the lawyer said that he had recently handled a similar case to mine and that he would make it impossible for Rob to find me. He got the ball rolling, and the divorce came through. Rob did ask my lawyer about where I was and that it would be possible for him to have my phone number. The lawyer was true to his word; he protected my anonymity. *Thank god!*

At nine months pregnant, all I wanted was the kid out. I was done with the pregnancy. I had gained so much weight that I was a walking tub. I was also beginning to have mood swings. I told my OB/GYN, and we decided that it was time that I was induced on May 21, 2002. I screamed at my OB/GYN. I told him that I was *not* going to have my child on my *mother's* birthday. John appeased me by asking if the twenty-second was better. I said yes. I guess the bottom line is it really did not matter, but in my mind, it did.

So <u>Samual Thomas Rifenberg</u> was born on <u>May 22, 2002</u>, at <u>nine pounds, two ounces,</u> at <u>11:58 p.m.</u> via <u>C-section.</u>

After a week of being in the hospital, we left for home, the apartment in Speculator. I was beginning to see a side of Thom I did not like. I was starting to feel like a single parent. I began to see what his kids were telling me. He was good at making babies but not good at helping with one. In the first three months of Sam's life, the only time I got help from Thom was when I needed to sleep. He would watch Sam long enough for me to have slept in three-hour increments because of breastfeeding. My body was getting run down, but my mind was worse. I was sinking into a deep despair.

The more disgruntled I got, the less time I spent with Thom. I commenced looking for another companion. I had long since recognized that I was bisexual. So I started looking for a girlfriend. I went to a dating site—which one, I don't remember. There was where I met Renee.

Renee Tietz

When Sam was three months old, we moved to Mitchell, South Dakota, because of Renee. She lived in Mitchell, South Dakota. We all joined her at her place at first. I fell hard for Renee. She was my Michael Geddes but female. I loved her so much that I agreed to live in a trailer for the first time in my life—panic attack and all. I found that the trailer was making me paranoid; I kept thinking that it would burst into flames. Thom did not help because he had seen one too many trailer fires to be comfortable in it.

I also discovered that I loved the woman's body thoroughly. Sex between Renee and me was great. When I am with a man, I must coax myself along, but with a woman, I feel free and wild. She could get a rise out of me much quicker than any man. Sometimes I feel like I prefer women rather than men. Renee made me feel alive and fulfilled. She took over with caring for Sam. What a novel idea! I had a partner who was willing to help.

Shortly after six months, we were there. I bought a house just outside of Mitchell. I must have loved Renee a great deal because I could not stand the flatness. It drove me batty. The longer we were together, the more Renee got aloof and unhappy. She wanted me to divorce Thom and be only hers. I refused. We parted ways. I was heartbroken, but I understood her motivations.

Thom wanted to go back to the Adirondacks in New York. I could not blame him there. I was tired of South Dakota myself. There was a reason why I had chosen Thom over Renee. It was a three-letter word: *Sam*. I recognized that no matter what I did, it was not fair for Sam if I divorced his father. Thom, after all, was Sam's dad. I did not want to deprive him of that. Thus, we left South Dakota in July 2004. Sam was two years old.

We made our way back to Chestertown, New York. We stayed at the Alp Horn Motel while we looked at houses to purchase. We saw one in Elizabethtown, New York, on the internet. We decided to see and buy it. The whole process took all of three days to achieve.

Elizabethtown, New York

Everything fell together. The house, the town, the Essex County mental health and Elizabethtown health centers—it was all set up. Thom's cardiologist was in Plattsburgh, and his primary care doctor was the same as mine. My ego puffed up. I thought I had done a great job getting everything set up. Sam had his own doctor too. I was very pleased until I looked at where I stood. I was on a high. I had just *purchased* a house with *cash*. I *bought* a car. I went *appliance shopping, spent $1,000* all in one day. On top of that, I took the family out to eat a lot.

Thom became moodier and moodier. He had started to retreat into his shell. It was like I had two kids, one old and one young, but both got into trouble frequently. Then it hit me like a ton of bricks: Dennis. He would be the answer to my prayers. Where was it? It took me a week, but I found his number. I was extremely excited. Memories came flooding back, and I found myself blushing like a teenager. I remembered the times I had spent in bed with him. He was very good. We matched each other well. I was high and very manic. So I called him.

Dennis — The Second Time Around

Dennis and I talked every day for two months straight. I was manic. I made a mess of the finances. I told Dennis about it. I was honest. We ended up in a three-way conversation—Dennis, Thom, and me.

I got worse. I was beginning to have missing time. I suggested to Thom that we needed a caretaker, someone to take care of the finances and provide a stable home environment for Sam. We both agreed that Dennis would work out well. This would free me up to better take care of Sam. So I thought, but my real intention was that I wanted someone to take care of Sam so I could kill myself. My disease had progressed to that extent. Things were getting bad inside of me. I was high as a kite. I had a hard time making decisions. Nothing seemed to matter to me anymore. I had sex on my brains as the mania deepen. I remembered why I drank heavily when I was much younger. Thom and I agreed; talking to Dennis became a priority. We did another three-way conversation with Dennis. I stated my case, and Thom did too. Sam was then only three years old.

In 2005, Dennis pulled into the driveway. I was overjoyed. He set foot in the house, and I screamed. Sam the dog came with him. I squealed when I saw Sam the dog. I gave Dennis a cursory hug and quickly turned my attention to Sam the dog. It made my day because Sam the dog protected me, comforted me, and watched over me when Dennis was gone from the house when we were in Kalamazoo. He did not let *anyone* hurt me, including my ex-husband.

I was breathless. I ushered Dennis and Sam the dog into the house. Then Sam the boy was officially introduced to "Papa Dennis." They took to each other like milk to cookies. Then Sam the boy got introduced to Sam the dog. Sam the boy's first reaction was "What ears!" and he pulled the ears! I groaned in perceived pain. I told Sam the boy never to pull doggie ears ever again. He has not to this day.

That night, Dennis and I made love. It made me realize something. I was and am truly bisexual. I loved Dennis, but Renee used to take my breath away. I have not since found a woman like Renee. So I contented myself with being with a man. When I was in South Dakota, I felt really complete because of both Thom and Renee, but that was all right; things didn't need to be perfect.

In 2014, Thom died of a heart attack. The last two years of his life, he became combative and showed signs of dementia. When he passed, I was grateful because the last year was difficult for him. One thing I admired Thom for was that he stepped back as a father and let Dennis be the "real" dad. Therefore, Sam was not unhappy when Thom died. Sam, by that time, had begun to think of Dennis as being his real dad.

Dennis and I honored Thom for a year. Then we made plans to get married. I loved Dennis deeply, and I wanted to have a church wedding. So during the school break, we took a trip to Las Vegas to get married. I had organized a wedding with one of the chapels there. No, it was not the Elvis Presley service. The package I chose was the first day we registered for the marriage. Then we had the service and the ride back to the hotel in a limousine.

I had a black dress with white trimmings on it. Dennis and Sam were in tuxedos. Things had never been so right as that day. We exchanged vows and headed back to the hotel. It was the perfect day. We went to see a show that evening to round the day off. The next day, we flew home. Dennis and I talked. We decided to have a mini reception at the halfway house near our house in Elizabethtown. We invited about twenty people whom we knew relatively well. That went off without a hitch. Everything went so well that it felt like it was meant to be.

Dennis and I were married on February 18, 2015. We have had a very prosperous marriage, but not everything has gone right. My mental illnesses have progressed. My dissociative identity disorder is becoming more pronounced. That is a nice way of saying that I can be a few people in one body. Then there is the bipolar, where I would swing from one pole (depression) to another pole (mania or elation). I also have the lovely posttraumatic stress disorder, which I inherited from how my Malaysian family had treated me. Borderline personality is also another that I landed with because of my childhood.

When all is said and done, I tried to commit suicide seven months ago in June 2019. I gave up. One of my personalities took over and downed a bottle of Benadryl. Something happened to me that night. I snapped and called for help. Thus, I was admitted into the Mental Health Unit. At this juncture, I must make a note. We were in the process of changing my medication, so the mental break was not a complete surprise.

I was in the "ward" for about eight days. They took what my psychiatric nurse was doing and ran with it. My medication was revamped. I noticed that I was feeling more alive and awake. I liken it to the movie *The Awakenings* because that was what it felt like for me. One day I was in a clouded stupor; the next, I was awake and living life. Still, all in all, I have become very functional because of Jennifer Kanaly's work (my psychiatric nurse).

The other positive thing that happened was that I integrated my most destructive personality, called No Name. Since then, I've heard one voice rather than multiple voices. My head used to be very crowded and noisy, a little bit like a restaurant I know called Texas Roadhouse. I had never known how much strength No Name had until we joined.

There are many people I need to thank for my getting through a very rough 2019. The two that stand out are Molly Jacobson and Jennifer Kanaly. The first six months of 2019 were extremely rough. The second half of the year was good. I need to thank Jennifer Kanaly, my psychiatric nurse, for her expertise in handling my case. She intuitively knows what to do with me. Then there is Molly Jacobson, my therapist, without whom the integration would not have gone so smoothly, if at all possible. Both have cared for and supported me through thick and thin.

The other person I need to express gratitude for is Dennis W., my husband. We have been through much together. I don't think I know a stronger, more self-assured, and more confident man than him. He makes the term "death do us part" seem easy and very meaningful.

More than anything else, I would like to say this: without the people above, the self-confident woman I am today would not exist. I am managing my life, my finances, and my work. This story is one of success—from a troubled childhood and the depths of despair to a very happy and normal life.

I wrote this in 2019 when things were just settling down. In June 2020, I started going back to work. My meds were again revamped because I had started to develop dystonic reactions to the meds I was taking, so I was switched to Latuda. I have now been on Latuda for almost a year and a half. I have not experienced anything like this in my life. Because of the effects of the drug, I have been incredibly stable for all that time *and* holding a full-time job at the same time. A lot of things have calmed down, and my stability is unsurpassed. I am a better mother and wife today than I have ever been.

I also have a dream now. I want to be the Dennis W. to other women like myself. I want to give them what Dennis gave me so freely—a life worth living, a spark that I never had or saw possible until now.

I will end by saying this: *thank you*, Dennis, my love, for being the person you are and the light in my darkness. Because of you, the sun is now shining brighter than ever. Thank you!

POEMS

Diamond

Trauma

Trauma, like the proverbial flu,
Passes
Growth—
       Like a maturing child
Embedded in me,
Never too young
To challenge the Darkness inside.
My Uncle shaped me
Like blackness creeping over the land
As I lost hope, dwelling in the dark.
But I will pick up the pieces
Of what I started thirty years ago,
Rebuilding the child within,
Reframing the memories of times past.
Let the light fill,
       Chasing the murkiness away.
Look at me.
I am Diamond.
I am a survivor.

 Soundless Night

Chest rising . . . falling,
Breathing.
    Inhale and exhale,
        Listening to the deafening noise of a soundless night,
           Air fresh with a light scent of the multitudes of Hibiscus.
Leave me alone, I thought
As the floor creaks.
Sadness . . . No.
Smell mixed with a strong scent of cheap cologne and muskiness of
manhood,
Hands—large, calloused, and chunky—on my stomach.
No . . . Uncle.
It hurts. Why?
Mama . . . Daddy.
Help me, please.
The unanswered cry of a child lost in the opaque of night.

Decisions

Go left or right?
One foot forward or not?
Decisions, decisions—
Bane of my life, like the lecture of a brother.
What do I know?
What do I not know?
Does it matter?
Everything washes away with water in the end.
Decisions—
Cannot live with them
Nor can I live without them.

Sleeplessness

Opaque as night,
Black as a room without lights,
Air . . . thick, crisp.
Crickets chirp.
Animals sleep.
But I am awake,
Like a deer caught in headlights.
Grateful slumber,
                    Where are you?
I need rest, lay down,
No toss nor turn—
Just be!

Mess after Meals

Cleaning—
Bane of my life.
Mess
Everywhere.
Smells like crisp, fresh green beans.
Need to start scrubbing.
Not certain how to contain
The mess/destruction of the kitchen.
"Put your back into it,"
My mother says.
Agreed—
        Attacks counters,
Muscles contracting, making headway,
Back spasming.
Finally,
Kitchen shines.
Cleaning ends.
Relief.

Time

Time flies
Like oozing sand in an hourglass.
Everything has its place,
Including sexual predators.
Time heals all wounds.
One day
There will be no more nightmares nor
Haunting memories.
In my dreams, that day is here,
Where there is freedom from pain—anguish—
And peace where flowers grow,
Where light is all encompassing and darkness
No more but a distant memory,
Tranquility an everyday occurrence.

Pin drop
Quiet—
    Soundless as
        Darkness blankets the house.
Time for bed.
Sleep,
    Dearest—to all a
Good night.

Trust

Looking back,
Men—
Too many to count, sexual predators.
Got hurt.
Trust suffers.
Learning how to trust again,
Growing, inside.
Progress as each day passes—
Modification complete.

Round
White
Tiny little miracles.
Pills drop
Into the bottle; shakes—
Sounds like bees in a hive, raging
As a bull at a rodeo,
Wild,
As going to the Disco, to drink, dance,
Attracting my senses, lulling me into a dreamlike state,
Catapulting my being to the unknown heavens.
Remember what they are! Pills!
Sobering,
Like a brand newly dry alcoholic.
Reality sinks in—
Pills no more.

Plagues

Rats coming out of the basement in droves,
Blessed running diseases on tiny feet.
Disgusting!
       Just like my childhood—
Rejecting the past like the plague it was,
Learning to deal with it,
Painstakingly slow but coming
       Out of the darkness,
Living in the present.
Today—no plagues,
No rats nor screams,
Just being
       In the moment,
Nothing untoward.
Blissful way of life.

In the Moment

Sitting down,
Lost in thought,
Brain in slow motion.
Mood
      Stable—consistent.
Deep breaths,
In and out.
Smells
      So good.
It reminds me
Of a fresh Summer's night.
Grateful
Past
      Not haunting anymore,
Quiet
Well-being,
Embracing present
      Like the dog with a bone,
Loving future
        Like silk sheets on a bed.
I am me.
I am
A Survivor.

Head:
> Resting in the palm of my hand,
>> Bowed, tired.

Night:
> Darkness, soundless, almost deafening,
>> Creeps over the land.

Light:
> Bright, breathing slower, more pronounced,
>> Rise and fall of the chest.
>>> Is this Serenity?

Mind quiet,
Just being in the moment.

Meetings

Inhaling the crisp night air—
Smells fresh as garden salad—
I stroll into the meeting place,
Filled with people regardless of creed or color.
Each eagerly waits for the bewitching hour to begin.
Individuals share
Their experience, strength, and hope,
Contributing to make men and women grateful
For little miracles in life.
Fantastic collection of humans,
Interesting, like an engrossing novel.
Meetings—
Nothing can replace it for this alcoholic.

Suicide

Numbness washes over me,
Like waves crashing on the beach.
My eyes shift toward the bottle—cylindrical object that houses pills.
Oh my!
Pouring into palm of my hand—
So many puny little wonders,
Admiring white, shiny specs.
Mouthwatering at the sight,
Numbness passing through me.
With mental anguish and pain,
I did it again, screaming soundlessly.
No . . .
The whole bottle.
Oh cripes!
What now?
Call Molly—panicking
Numbness coursing through me.
"Hello?"
"This is Jesse."
Wrong person.
Forgive me. I did it again!

#

Posttraumatic Stress Disorder—
Diagnosis that plagues my soul,
Derails logical thinking,
Bending my mind into a pretzel,
Ignores present,
Embraces past.
Flashbacks galore—
Slowly reframing memories,
Finally accepting the diagnosis,
Moving forward
With strength, faith,
Hope.

Parents

Emotional upheaval
Lies in relation to my parents' warring relationship,
Trauma akin to rape visited upon me because of it.
Mother always crying
              At everything no matter the issue or subject,
Father amused and toyed with Mom's presumed weakness.
Mother feels culpable and poor, making ends meet with difficulty.
Father, rich, throws money like the unending tomorrows on frivolous
things—
Mother gentle, soft-spoken, like holding a toddler in arms,
Dad venomous as a snake, careless, blustery, and unjust.
They quarreled all the time,
              Punctuated only by Dad's shouts and Mom's tears—
Always without respect, berating each other mercilessly,
Disagreements that tormented me in my childhood,
Thrown in between the two,
Like a tug-of-war rope, with each on his/her own end—pulling.
Mom tugs at the unknowing, innocent child that I was.
Dad hauls on the other side,
Always abrupt with anger.
Mom would share sweet nothings, knowing full well that I would
tell Dad.
He would be angry at the so-called sweet nothings that Mom relayed
through me.

Innocence lost

As I was caught in the middle of a brutal, infinite conflict.

I screamed, "Get out of my head!" There was no response from either.

Cruel awakening

                  Bestowed upon me by my lovely, heartfelt Parents.

Ice Storm

Trees droop,
    Glistening as
        Everything is
            Encased in ice.
Nervous tension—
    Teeth clenched,
        Body and shoulders taut,
            Arms flexed,
                Hands on wheel, gripped until knuckles white.
Such is the drive home in an ice storm—
    Wheels turning,
        Car slipping, sliding,
            Wind gusts belting the car,
                Roads icy and unforgiving,
                    Every muscle tight
                        like a compressed spring.
Ah, my driveway, out of the mess.
Happiness—I am home!

Admiration

Attractive,
    Contemplative,
        Understanding,
            Level-headed,
                Intelligent,
                    Stubborn
Are some words that describe the man I love.
    Meaningful,
        Thoughtful,
           Loving
Are attributes that he so plainly displays without cognizance.
He is the sweetest, most endearing man I know.

Without You

Without you, I would be lost in the emptiness of a galaxy.
Without you, my heart would bleed endlessly.
Without you, joy is inert with no meaning.
Without you, my change would be incomplete.
My love, my solar system . . .
You are my world, my soul, my everything.
With you, the universe bursts into living color.
With you, my heart skips a beat in anticipation.
With you, my life is ever blessed.
My love, my solar system . . .
You are my world, my soul, my everything!

The Voice That Embraces

A voice whispers in the dark of night,
"I know you."
Arms snake around my sides—
Warm,
      Cozy feelings as well as utter and complete safety;
Scent
      Musky, a delightful, intoxicating strength
That wrap you up in an eternal glee,
Joyous and carefree.
Is this what it's like to have
A voice that whispers in the dark of night,
"I know you"?
You are me.
The voice that almost never was
Is now alive,
Robust and well.
A year ago, I could not hear or feel you,
But now
The sky is not the limit.
It is time for the voice to step forward
And live
      Like the voice that shouts,
"I know you."

Depression

As I stare out into space,
My stomach lurches.
My heart bleeds.
Sadness washes over me
Like water on glass.
Ah . . . my dearest friend has come to visit.
Its name is Depression.
Smiling is a chore—
Losing interest in living,
Sorrow an everyday occurrence
Where there is no joy,
Only despondency.
Life is like South Dakota,
Where most of everything is one level—flat.
My only hope is in this affirmation:
"This too shall pass."

Flu Bug

Bone weariness fills my all.
Spine tingling chills my body,
Weight heavy on my shoulders.
I feel depleted from fighting this bug,
Low-grade fever all day long.
Such is a touch of the flu bug,
Tiredness so pronounced
That it takes everything I have just to move—
Nose stuffed and congested,
Sinuses plugged,
Eyes watering and pressured, creating a ginormous headache.
Enough already—this bug must run its course.
Sigh . . . fatigue seems to be my best friend.

COVID-19

Words have no meaning
As I watch you move from me.
Six feet apart at all times—
Is that fair?
I see you, but now you are
A figment of my imagination.
"Social distancing"—
Two words I am learning to hate.
It hurts.
Is this meant to be?
Deaths
          Too many to count
Fear
      Of a virus
                A blasphemous idea,
Riddled in every Man,
Woman, and
Child.
Am I to live?
Or die?
God only knows.

My Dearest Love

You are my Orb
That lights in the Blackness of the tunnel I walk in.
You float with ease through the Darkness of night.
You can burst into the brightness of a gazillion suns.
You are my knight in shining armor.
Life erupts into vivid color when you are near.
My Dearest Love,
Nobody can replace you.
You are my sky, moon, and star.
You are ever attentive at my side.
My world would be lost without you.
You are my everything!

Alcoholism

Smells
     Pungent,
          Like vomit.
Atmosphere
        Dark, dank, obscure,
           With a heaviness that sits on you for days on end.
Time stops.
Bar sticky
      From spilt beer.
He leans over and whispers,
"You're done. Come!"
     Swings around.
           There he is.
  Blood Rushed to my head in
     Embarrassment.
My inner voice screaming, "*No!*"
     Walking beside him to the door,
Realizing in a split second of clarity
My Dearest Friend
        Alcohol is No More.
Stumbling out the entrance,
I recoiled,
     Sunlight almost blinding
As he ushered me to the car.

Deep, Utter Sadness
 Enveloped my being
As we leave the Bar—
For what?
 Hope, Health, and Clean Living—
Peace?

In the Dark of Night

Mama . . . Daddy . . .
Where are you?
The question that reverberates through the darkness.
Creak, Creak.
The noise of unwanted footsteps.
Blackness.
No . . .
He is coming.
        As the floor squeaks under each weighted step of a big six-foot
full-grown man.
No . . .
What can I do?
Nothing.
I am nine, and he is old.
He has power, not me.
No . . . As the door swings open,
He turned the TV off.
Closer and closer—
He is now a three-dimensional shape.
Menacingly, he covered my mouth.
Screaming does no good.
I felt the fight left me.
All I know is
It hurts!

My Husband

Memories
Flood my being
As darkness creeps over the land,
Enveloping it with blackness
That is completely devoid of light.
Yet
In the distance lies a glimmer
Of radiance so bright
And comforting,
Like the embrace of
A mother consoling her child—
Love
So freely given,
Companionship as none
Can compare.
Thank you,
My Love,
For chasing the darkness
Away from
My Soul, Body, and Mind.

My Friend Annie, the Wheelchair Bound

Do you see me?
Yes, I do.
Do you hear me?
Yes, maybe, I think.
Here is a bite of food.
Uhh . . . Uhh . . . Uhh.
Here comes the airplane, in for the landing!
Where is the dignity?
I see you,
But I do not understand you.
I hear you,
But I know not what you say
Uhh . . . Uhh . . . Uhh.
Is it hard to be trapped in an unresponsive body?
The intelligence so easily apparent.
Even if you are wheelchair bound,
You are part of the human race—
Often misunderstood.

My Dearest Love

Reaching out to touch your image in my mind
As my eyes close,
Gently caressing the rough yet soft facial whiskers,
Feeling an indescribable warmth flush throughout my whole body,
Depth of which puts a lump in your throat.
I could feel tears welling up.
Is this Love?
I am not sure.
All I know is you are a part of me.
I feel you.
See you.
Need you!
We are dancers in the tango of life.
Today and Always,
My Love,
Friend, and Lover.

Duke, my Dog

They say
>   Eyes are the window

To your soul.
What do mine say?
Duke . . .
It hurts.
You are part of my soul,
Not just a dog.
You taught me about life,
>   Love,

How to be Loved.
You put the "z" in Zest.
Now you are gone . . .
I am crushed.
All I can think of
>   Is the line from *Black Beauty*:

"Twill all be right some day or night."
Goodbye, my Friend.
>   As my heart breaks.

Grief

Duke . . .
The soundless cry that reverberates in my soul.
My heart aches
In waves.
Seems grief,
            Like my ever-present friend,
Shreds my spirit into a gazillion pieces.
Ah, Duke . . .
Tears welling up
        As psychic pain rips through my chest.
So young,
But the depth of your love lessons is Immeasurable.
You sit and gaze into my eyes with adoration.
Feels like I could do anything,
Everything to you,
And all will be all right.
Your Love and Trust rock me.
My Hope,
One day I could love as you do,
My dog,
My dearest Friend.

I am only human.
With a broken heart.
Farewell.

My Heart Aches

Duke . . .
What a teacher you are!
Pain,
    Like being kicked in the stomach,
        Is an ever-abiding friend.
You did for me
What I could not have done for myself.
You broke the dam within.
All my life,
I stuffed all my emotions
Regardless of what they are.
I built a fortified dam.
Duke . . .
You broke that dam.
Now
My heart bleeds endlessly.
I do not know how to stop.
You hit me where it hurts.
And I grieve
        For you but also
For the broken child within.
Duke . . .
Go with God.
Diamond . . .
There is Light.

Dearest, Dad

I see you.
But our paths
Diverge.
You are Father/Dad.
But I know you not.
You glared.
I cringed,
So much so that I can taste
Fear.
Your voice booms.
My heart races.
Did I do something wrong?
Your wit quick—
I always admired.
Some of the time,
You looked distracted,
And I wondered what it means.
Even though I know you not,
Your abiding Love is apparent.
Oft times
I could almost feel your guidance,
Even from beyond the grave.
You are a big part of my spiritual being.
Rest easy, Dad.

A lump lodged in my throat.
Your daughter is well,
Just as you always
Thought and believed!

My Friend – An Alcoholic Mania

Past Alcoholism re-emerged.
When I passed by the liquor store the other day,
Something made me gaze longingly at the entrance.
The seeds of Mania from Bipolar Disorder burst
Into Living color—
Energy
    In Abundance,
Sleep
    A forgotten Commodity,
Spending Sprees.
Ah . . . "Hello, Darkness, my old friend."
The line from a song by Simon and Garfunkel, "The Sound of Silence"—
Darkness
       Like a Long Lost friend,
Revisited.
Sigh . . .
       Nice to be able to breathe
A sigh of relief.
"Hello, Darkness, my old friend."
You need not stay with me again—
Or ever,
For that matter.

What Limits?

They say,
"Sky's the limit."
I say,
"Why limit yourself?"
There is a whole universe of possibilities out there
To participate in.
Why limit yourself to just the sky?
I used to think
My mental disability was all I had,
All I was—
Not true!
Every man, woman, child
Is a myriad of possibilities.
The only roadblock
Is one's own thoughts and beliefs.
I say, "Roadblock be damned."
I once lived in the constraints of others.
I once allowed others to dictate
My thoughts and action.
That girl is no more.
I now stand by my convictions and the limitless
Potential
Outside the proverbial box.
I ask you

Not what is but why not?
The only barriers that exist
Are the ones placed there by ourselves.
Why not burst out?
The potential is again
Limitless.

Past Teachers

Dad . . .
Rajiv . . .
Duke . . .
Grizz, Thor, Freki, Snowy . . .
A myriad of people and dogs
That have graced my life.
One thing they all have in common
Is how they have moved me profoundly.
My father—I admired his accomplishments from afar.
Rajiv, my nanny,
Showed me how to love a child
That was not his own.
Duke, my dog, was my teacher;
He taught me how to grieve.
Grizz, Thor, Freki, and Snowy
Convinced me that unconditional love existed.
All these people and dogs
Have not just affected me intensely
But also given
A piece of themselves to me.
Today
I can feel deeply
Because of these fine instructors.
I have no idea what the future holds,

But I do know that
I am a better person
Because of the lessons of my past
Loves.

Then and Now

Shadows of the past
Revisited—
No longer a bystander
In the game of Life,
Emotions riled.
"Mirror, mirror on the wall,
Who is the fairest of them all?"
A line from *Snow White*.
I look into the mirror.
I do not see "the fairest of them all."
For that matter,
Never used to like the mirror in any respect.
What changed?
A little patience with Self,
Acknowledgement of shortcomings,
Understanding one's hardships,
With a dash of gentleness toward Self.
"It is all right"—
Something that I was never able to say until now.
Today
I can puff my chest out and say,
"Give me what you got, Life."
"I'm Ready"—
Echoes of an almost forgotten

SpongeBob.
Much has resolved;
Some stayed the same.
Above all else,
I have my dignity,
Grace, and
Peace
What more can I ask?

Racism

On my way to work,
I pass by a paddock
With a host of Black Angus cows.
In the middle of the herd
Stands one Red Angus bull.
I am that Bull,
Mixed in a Sea of white faces.
Do I feel different?
Certainly—but not uncomfortable,
For I am human
Among many.
What then is the differentiation other than
Skin color?
None.
If I were ill, you could
Give me an organ to save my life
If our blood types matched.
How then do we differ?
Racial Injustice
Is borne in a minority
Who is a part of the majority—
A misguided few
Setting an unfair tone for all.
How do we combat this?

Heaven only knows.
Education plays a role
In the end.
Eyes must be opened
To the realization.
Ideas are just that.
Reality, however, is
Far more prosaic.
We must come to an understanding
That segregation
Is no longer Acceptable,
For we belong
To only one race.
That is
The Human Race.

Gratitude

Waking up,
Crisp first light,
Registering that it was Sunday morning—
Cold,
Making my nose twitch as it
Sends a chill down my spine.
One more shift;
Then a break
Finally,
Many thoughts running
Through my head—
Black and Red Anguses, Work, Husband, Son,
Most of all
Gratitude
To have made it this far without
Losing everything or
Having to compromise,
The ever-present Bipolar
Still an issue,
Albeit better controlled.
Thank you, Jennifer Kanaly,
For saving my Soul
And giving me back
My Life.

PTSD – Once Upon a Time

Sadness envelopes my being
As memories of a forgotten past
Resurface to haunt my very soul.
What appears as a harmless
Display of affection
Belies an ugly truth.
A man/an uncle
Respected as a leader and Imam
Or priest from the Islamic faith
Molests,
Rapes
A ten-year-old girl/child
Who understood naught
On the topic of sex.
Where is the justice?
Many Moons later,
The girl became a woman,
Dreams of those heinous acts
Of a wolf in sheep's clothing.
I am now fifty.
At times,
I am ten again.
"How do I heal?"
A question that reverberates

In the soundless night.
The depth of the sadness
Is so pronounced
That you can see
The rippling effect throughout
My adult life.
A touch, word, or sound
Can teleport me
Back to the sensations,
Emotions, or
Sounds of those times,
Like a flash.
Sigh . . .
My hope is that
One day
The memories
Will lose their charge
And power.

Parent-Child Paths of Enlightenment

"Never"—
What an interesting
Word.
"I am Never wrong,"
Screams my Dad through
The recesses of a near empty house.
"I will Never be happy
Thanks to your Father,"
Cries my Mother.
Time and time again,
I stare in the mirror,
And I recognize my parents in me.
I also see the past hurt
In the Reflected image,
Eyes moist and Sad,
Filled with unshed tears.
Mother says,
"You are just like your Dad!"
Relatives say,
"You are your Mother's Daughter!"
I say
I am both and

None.
I am the product of
Choices
Made by my parents.
Neither
Would admit their mistakes,
Which brings us to the adage
"Pride comes before a Fall."
For me, however,
Pride comes before a bruising.
It is sad how
Children pay for their parents' preferences
And blunders,
Especially when the adults in that child's life
Are thoughtless.
May I always
Be mindful of My Choices
As my son travels down the
Path to adulthood.

Forgotten Pain

I gaze into the mirror.
A ten-year-old girl/child
Stares back—
Her eyes haunted,
Head bowed
As her shoulders shake
From uncontrolled sobbing,
Robbed of her will to live
Yet ghosting along relentlessly.
In her mind's eye,
She dreams of a day
Where she no longer hurts.
How do you recover
From plundered innocence
That was lost
At the hands
Of a well-respected Priest/Imam
Whose behavior was akin to a bloodthirsty vampire?
I carry that hurt
'til this day and probably
For the rest of my life.
Now I hear of another
Predator whose smile
Belies an evil within.

The anger at this man
Simmers like a dormant
Volcano, ready to burst.
In a way, I wish I could see him
Because he will finally gaze at a woman
That possesses a fierce conviction
Where predators like him
Will be brought to justice.
A violent part of me
Wants to tear him
From limb to limb for those perpetrated crimes
That he committed on my best friend's daughters.
As attractive as the thought can be,
Revenge poisons the soul.
Justified might the rage be,
It tarnishes even the purest of intent.
I need to be able to say to
The ten-year-old girl/child,
"It is all right, truly."
Time may not heal all wounds,
But it sure mends
The soul like a seamstress
Working magic on an evening gown.
Someday that gown will be
Complete!

A Learning Experience

Echoes of a young woman's voice
That mirrors my own
Reverberate in the silence of my mind.
I hear you.
I feel you.
We are not dissimilar,
You and I
You know me not.
For everybody's sake, it is probably best
That you do not know me.
It hurts to be limited in one's behavior
Or to have acceptable parameters or rules,
But trust not in the system but in your higher power or self.
Knowledge is power, yes.
It can also be a curse.
I see your path.
It is fraught with obstacles.
I want to reach out and say gently say,
"Try this or that,"
But it is not my place.
Acceptance is a bitter pill at times.
I understand, however, that some things
Are placed by your higher power
To teach you that patience is a virtue,

One that is hard fought
And hard won.
May the powers that be Bless
Your and my
Paths.

My Bipolar Lot

I sit and watch an Asian woman
All these fifty years,
Always up and then down—
Heavens
Or hell,
No in-between—
Very tiring, not to mention frustrating.
Normalcy—
A rare commodity.
How do I trust myself
When oft times I find me
Hard to comprehend,
Let alone make sense of?
My zest in life
Seemed to have zipped out the door!
How do I cope?
What do I need to do?
My son is learning to care for himself.
My husband is succeeding in his endeavors,
Be it gardening or whatever.
Me—
Where am I?
I want to live, but
Please, somebody,

Show me a path of least resistance.
Fog and Haze—
I am lost.
Please let me be found.

The Emerging Road

The most wonderful day of my life was
When I had a bouncing baby boy—
Nine pounds, two ounces, with a scream
That you can hear
All the way to the other side
Of the maternity ward.
I knew my life was forever altered.
Now, nineteen years later,
I am at the same crossroads.
This time, I have a choice:
Life with managed mental health
Or an untimely demise by my own hand.
I choose life.
With that choice comes fear,
Like the one when I first held my son
For the first time in my life.
The future is opaque,
Unclear.
The road is no longer straight
And narrow.
It seems that there is a convergence
In my path.
The various lanes
I have taken have led me here.

What is ahead, I know not.
As worrisome as that is,
It is also exciting.
I can finally say
I want to live
Not for anyone else but
Myself.
The determination to succeed
Against all odds
Is all mine;
I greedily protect it.
May the wonders of this world and the next
Bless this sacred trail.

Father's Day Wishes

I have watched you grow
From being a father
To a dad.
My son is not yours,
But you are the only
Dad he has really known intimately.
Fifteen years have passed.
He still looks at you
The same way he did when
He first laid eyes on you
At the tender age of three.
He loves you immensely
With a depth that
Pays no regard to biology.
Consequently, he has matured
Into a confident young man.
He makes mistakes.
You teach him how
To live with
And overcome them.
There is no better Dad
Than a Sincere,
Honest,
Loving

Stepfather.
Happy Father's Day, Sweetheart.
My Gratitude—
Also heartfelt thanks!

A Life's Work

I . . .
Am . . .
A Guide . . .
All that I have been through in this life
Has led me to this.
A Vision of Love
And Heart
Brought me here.
I go by many phrases—
"The blind man's dog,"
"Lantern in the dark,"
"Hope to the downtrodden."
I . . .
Have been where you are.
My purpose is clear.
I may not understand,
But I stand corrected.
I invite you on this journey
As you are a part of it.
At thirteen years of age,
I was given a dream.
I saw my father's house fall
Under the constellation Leo.
The mighty Lion's power

Forced
My father's legacy
To the ground.
The trembling mansion
Flattened
Like Squished Sardines
In a can.
Today, at fifty,
I see this dream
Graced by my Higher Power
As the path for my life's work,
No more
The mild, subservient
Malaysian Girl.
I see what Life
Has turned me into—
The Tiny Flower among the grass
Where Her beauty
Once bloomed,
Never invisible.
I am the ending
Of an era
With a promise
Of a new beginning,
Ours.
Dear Friends,
As a kind,
Compassionate individual
Was once for me—
He gave me Hope
Where there was only Despair—
I . . .
Could Be . . .
Your . . .
Guide . . .

A Beacon of Light
In Our
Imperfect World!

Printed in Great Britain
by Amazon